Essential Science

Light
&
Seeing

Peter Riley

FRANKLIN WATTS

This edition 2010.

First published in 2006 by Franklin Watts
338 Euston Road, London NW1 3BH

Franklin Watts Australia
Hachette Children's Books
Level 17/207 Kent Street, Sydney NSW 2000

Editor: Rachel Tonkin
Designer: Proof Books
Picture researcher: Diana Morris
Illustrations: Ian Thompson

Picture credits:
Chris Butler/SPL: 6; Macduff Everton/Corbis: 13cl;
Gallo Images/Corbis: 25; Greatshots Ltd/Photolibrary: 15t;
Cindy Kassab/Corbis: 5; David Parker/SPL: 26cr;
Adam Peiperl/Corbis: 1, 19cl; Neal Preston/Corbis: 27;
Charles O'Rear/Corbis: 4; Roger Ressmeyer/Corbis: 9;
Alan Schein Photography/Corbis: 21c;
Mark Thomas/SPL: 21t; Craig Tuttle/Corbis: 26bl, 29br;
Ron Watts/Corbis: 10b; Roger Wood/Corbis: 13tr;
Chris Fairclough: 17.

All other images: Andy Crawford

With thanks to our model Josie Cook and Tiaki Losa

Every attempt has been made to clear copyright.
Should there be any inadvertent omission please
apply to the publisher for rectification.

A CIP catalogue record for this book
is available from the British Library

ISBN 978 0 7496 9603 0

Dewey Classification: 535

Printed in Malaysia

Franklin Watts is a division of Hachette Children's Books,
an Hachette UK company.
www.hachette.co.uk

CONTENTS

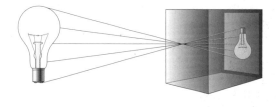

LIGHT AND SEEING

You can see the words on this page because there is light around you. If there was no light, it would be dark and you would not be able to see anything at all.

Light travels from this page into your eyes but the page is not producing the light. The light comes from a light source which is reflected into your eyes off the paper. If you are reading this in the day the light source is the Sun. If you are reading at night, the light source is most probably an electric lamp.

Electric lamps provide light for us to see at night.

The path of light

Light usually travels in straight lines. You can see this when sunlight shines through a gap in your bedroom curtains in the morning. The light shines on the dust particles in the air in the room and is reflected into your eyes. You see a beam of light with straight edges crossing the room.

Shadows

If you look around you, you can probably see areas that are darker than others. They are in shadows cast by other objects. Shadows are darker because there is not as much light present. The light travelling in straight lines has been stopped by an object.

You can see the straight edges of the beams of sunlight in this picture.

Data

When scientists do experiments, they make observations and record them. This information is called data. It may be in the form of a table, bar chart or line graph.

Look around your home and make a list of the light sources in each room. Find a total for each room and make a bar chart like the one shown here. How does your bar chart compare to this one?

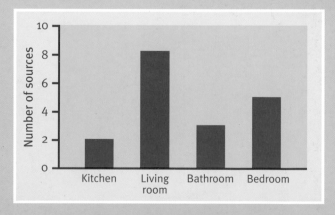

You will find data on many pages in this book. Can you answer the questions on it? Answers to the questions are on page 31.

SOURCES OF LIGHT

Only a few objects give out light. They are called light sources, or luminous objects. The Sun, candles and electric lamps are all light sources.

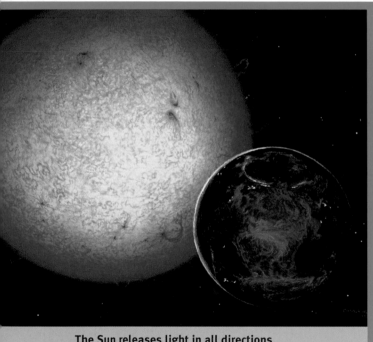

The Sun releases light in all directions into space. Some of it reaches the Earth.

The Sun and stars

The Sun is made from a huge ball of gases. At its centre the force of gravity crushes one of the gases, called hydrogen, so hard that it changes into another gas called helium. When this happens, light energy is released. The Sun is a star and all the stars in the Universe produce light in the same way.

Burning

When something, such as a candle, burns, it takes part in a chemical change with oxygen in the air. During this change light energy is released.

The brightness of stars

Astronomers use a scale to measure the brightness of stars. They call it a scale of magnitude. A star with a magnitude of 0 is very bright while a star with a magnitude of 6 is so dim it can only just be seen by the naked eye. Stars with magnitudes lower than this can only be seen with telescopes. Here are the magnitudes of five stars.

Mebsuta 3, Mirphak 1.8, Sheliak 4, Mira 9, Hamal 2

1 Arrange the stars in order starting with the brightest.
2 Which star cannot be seen by the naked eye?

The light bulb

A light bulb has a coiled metal wire inside, called a filament. It is a conductor of electricity but it has a high resistance. This means that the electricity has to push hard to get through. As the electricity pushes its way through the filament it makes the metal release energy in the form of heat and light.

filament

When electricity flows through the filament, light shines out from the lamp.

Fluorescent lights and screens

Some materials, called fluorescent materials, produce light when they receive energy from electricity. Television and computer screens and many strip lamps have fluorescent materials in them that glow when they are switched on.

Luminous objects

Objects which give out light are called luminous objects. Objects which do not give out light are called non-luminous objects. Most objects are non-luminous. We see them by the light that is reflected from them by luminous objects. For example, look at your hand. It is not glowing and making light like a luminous object. It is reflecting light from a luminous object, probably the Sun or an electric lamp.

The burning wax releases light energy. The light is reflected off non-luminous objects around the candle.

WHEN LIGHT TRAVELS

Light travels in straight lines but when it hits many objects its path is blocked and a shadow forms.

Keeping straight on

You can show that light travels in a straight line with a simple experiment. Cut a slit in a piece of card and place it in front of a torch. Point the torch across a piece of paper and switch it on. It should make a beam with straight sides.

> Light beams move in straight lines.

The pinhole camera

A camera also shows that light travels in straight lines. You can make a simple camera out of a box, silver foil and some tracing paper. Cut away one end of the box and replace it with silver foil. Replace the opposite end with tracing paper. Finish off the camera by making a hole with a pin in the middle of the foil. When the foil end of the box is pointed at a luminous object, such as a lamp, a picture of the lamp is seen on the tracing paper. The picture of the object is upside down.

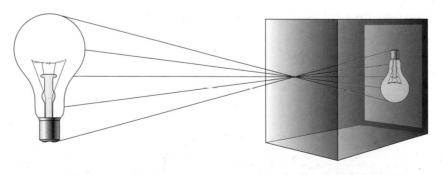

> Light passes from the object straight through the pin hole and makes a picture, called an image, on the tracing paper screen.

The speed of light

Light travels at 300,000 metres per second. When you switch on a lamp, the room seems to fill instantly with light but there is a tiny fraction of a second when it is still dark. However, the time is too short for our eyes to detect it.

The Sun is so far away from us that light takes about eight minutes to reach us. If someone could turn the Sun off like a lamp, we would not know until eight minutes later. Stars are much further from Earth. It takes years for their light to reach us.

Beams and rays

The columns of light we see shining through clouds or gaps in curtains are called beams. When scientists want to draw diagrams of how light moves they draw arrows, which they call light rays. You can think of light rays as being very thin beams of light and light beams as being made up of many parallel light rays.

Many stars are so far away it takes their light hundreds of years to reach the Earth.

Light years

The distance travelled by light in a year is called a light year. Here are some stars and their distances from the Earth in light years.

1 When an astronomer looks at the light from Altair tonight, in which year did the light leave the star?
2 In which year will light leaving Deneb now reach us?
3 How much closer to the Earth is Capella than Betelgeuse?

Star	Distance in light years
Altair	16
Betelgeuse	310
Capella	42
Deneb	1,800

SHADOWS

When a light ray is stopped by an opaque object, a shadow forms on the other side of the object. A shadow is dark because light is absent.

The shadow is connected to the part of the person touching the ground but does not show any of the person's features.

Shadow shapes

A shadow has a similar shape to the object which makes it. Light cannot bend round the sides of the object and make the shadow smaller or a different shape. The edge of the shadow is made by beams of light which just pass over the object's surface. They make an outline of the object in the space behind it. The outline is similar to the outline of the object.

In the shadow

You cannot see any details within a shadow. Features of the object such as its colour, patterns, writing or even a face cannot be seen in the shadow. All that can be seen is a region of darkness, which means that light is absent.

You can see the shadow cast by these clouds on the hills below.

Where shadows begin

If light is shone on an object that is on the ground or a table, a shadow forms which is connected to the object. It begins by the base of the object. If light is shone on an object in the air, such as sunlight shining on a cloud or a bird, the shadow is not connected to the object. It forms a dark region below the object, which has the object's outline.

Change in shadow length

When the light shining on the object from one side is high, it makes a short shadow. As the light is lowered, the length of the shadow increases. The length of the shadow depends on the height of the light shining on the object.

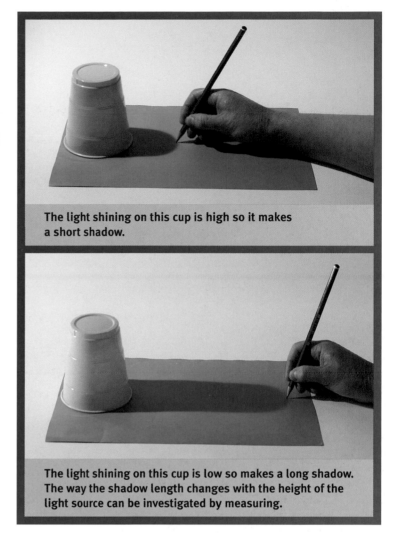

The light shining on this cup is high so it makes a short shadow.

The light shining on this cup is low so makes a long shadow. The way the shadow length changes with the height of the light source can be investigated by measuring.

The changing shadow

The data in the bar chart shows how the length of the shadow of an object changed with the height of the light source.

1 What is the length of the shadow when the light source is (a) 20 cm high; (b) 26 cm high?

2 When a shadow is 5 cm long, how high is the light source?

3 When the light source is 18 cm high, will the shadow be longer or shorter than when it was at a height of 20 cm?

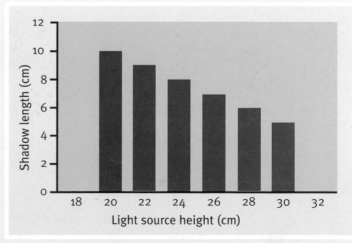

SHADOWS AND TIME

The Sun seems to move steadily across the sky every day. The shadows cast by objects in its light can be used to measure time.

The turning Earth

The Earth turns around on its axis once every 24 hours. As the Earth turns, parts of its surface come into the sunlight and then move out of it again. During this time, the Sun seems to rise in the sky until midday then sinks again before it sets. It is the turning Earth that makes the Sun seem to move.

Shadows and direction

When the Sun rises in the sky in the east, the shadows shorten and point towards the west. At midday the short shadows point towards the north in the Northern Hemisphere and towards the south in the Southern Hemisphere. As the Sun sinks in the sky in the west, the shadows lengthen and point towards the east.

As the Sun moves across the sky, the length and direction of shadows change. Never look at the Sun as it is so bright it can blind you.

Measuring time

The movement of the Sun across the sky means that shadows are produced in an orderly way and can be used to tell the time.

The Sun bar was a T-shaped object used by the Ancient Egyptians to tell the time. The Sun bar was held towards the Sun and the length of the shadow cast by the top of the T onto markings on the long bar was observed.

The sundial was used up until more recent times in many places in the world. As the direction of the shadows change they move across the surface of the sundial on which hours are marked.

The shadow is cast on a sundial by a long piece of metal called a gnomon. The time on this sundial is before four o'clock.

This Ancient Egyptian carving shows a man holding out a Sun bar. The change in length of the shadows are measured on the bar which is a long piece of wood with hours marked on them.

Sun and shadows

The length and direction of shadows were measured when the Sun was in different parts of the sky.

1 Fill in the gaps in the table by making predictions.

2 In which hemisphere were the observations made?

Sun's position	Shadow length (cm)	Shadow direction
East	50	West
South east	40	
	25	North
South west		N. East
	50	East

MATERIALS AND LIGHT

When light shines on most materials some of the light is absorbed and some of it is reflected. However, there are materials which allow light to pass through them. These materials transmit light.

Opaque materials

Most materials are opaque materials. When light strikes their surface, some of the light energy is absorbed and some is reflected. No light passes through them. They do not transmit light. On the unlit side of the material there is a region of darkness which makes a shadow.

The book is made from an opaque material. Light cannot pass through so the light shines on one orange and not the other.

The smooth surface of a transparent material, such as a glass, also reflects a little light. If it did not you would not be able to see the glass.

Transparent materials

Some materials transmit light. When light strikes their surface, a little is reflected but most passes straight through the material. This means that you can see clearly through a transparent material. The light rays pass through in parallel lines. As some light does not pass through the material there is a pale region on the unlit side which forms a shadow. It is much lighter than the shadow made by an opaque material.

Translucent materials

Translucent materials let light through, but you cannot see through them as you can with transparent materials. This is because the light rays do not pass through in parallel lines, as they do in transparent materials. When light is transmitted through a translucent material the light rays scatter in all directions. This makes it impossible to see clearly through a translucent material. Not all the light striking a translucent material passes through it, some is reflected and a little is absorbed by the material. This means that translucent materials make darker shadows than transparent materials.

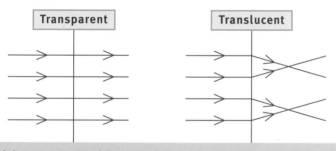

Light rays pass straight through transparent materials in parallel lines. As light rays pass through translucent materials, they scatter in different directions.

Some windows and doors have translucent glass in them so that they can let light in but people cannot see through them.

Identify the material

A light meter measures the amount of light in a certain place. The amount of light passing through a material was measured with a light meter and the data presented as a bar graph.

1 Which material was opaque?
2 Which material was transparent?
3 Which material was translucent?
4 Did A or C cast the darker shadow?

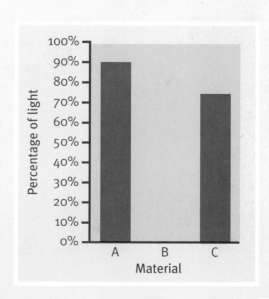

REFLECTING LIGHT

When a beam of light strikes most surfaces, a great deal of the light is reflected. If the surface is very smooth we see a picture in it called a reflection.

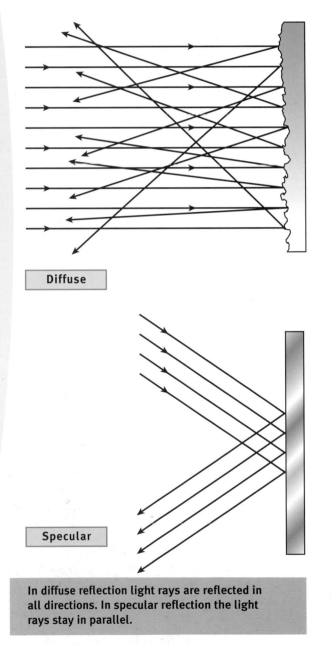

Diffuse

Specular

In diffuse reflection light rays are reflected in all directions. In specular reflection the light rays stay in parallel.

Diffuse reflections

The surfaces of most objects are not completely flat. They have tiny projections on them that stick up and make the surface uneven or slightly rough. When a beam of light strikes the surface, the light rays are reflected in all directions. This kind of reflection is called diffuse reflection.

Specular reflections

The surface of glass or water is very smooth and flat and does not have any projections. This means that when a beam of light strikes it, the light rays do not scatter. They are reflected from the surface in parallel lines. This type of reflection is called specular reflection.

Reflection and image

Some of the rays of light moving from the surface of any object travel in parallel lines. When they strike a smooth, flat surface, they are reflected in parallel lines, too. This makes them seem to appear in the object. This picture is called a reflection or image. The reflection is not an exact copy of the object. The left side of the object appears on the right and the right side on the left. We say that the image is the reverse of the object.

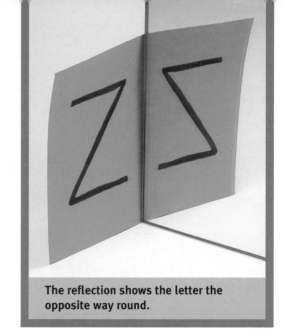

The reflection shows the letter the opposite way round.

Diffuse reflection occurs at the surfaces of the objects in this room. The light is reflected in all directions.

Can you see a reflection?

Make a prediction about whether a clear reflection of a lamp can be seen in the following surfaces then check by looking at the different surfaces under a lamp.

Surface	Reflection (yes/no)
This book cover	
This page	
Polished metal	
Wool pullover	

FLAT MIRRORS

Flat mirrors, sometimes called plane mirrors, are used to investigate how light rays are reflected. Plane mirrors can be used together to make a periscope or a kaleidoscope.

Rays and angles

When scientists study the reflection of light they use special terms to describe the rays and the paths they take. They call the ray which strikes the mirror the incident ray and the ray which is reflected the reflected ray. When they draw a diagram of an incident and reflected ray they draw a vertical line between them called the normal. The angle that the incident ray makes with the normal is called the angle of incidence and the angle the reflected ray makes with the normal is called the angle of reflection.

When a light ray strikes a flat mirror and is reflected, the angle of incidence is the same as the angle of reflection.

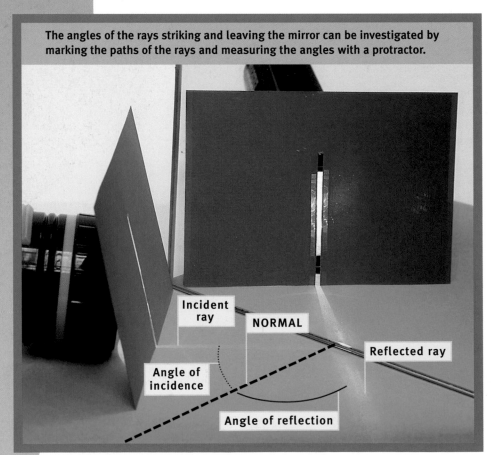

The angles of the rays striking and leaving the mirror can be investigated by marking the paths of the rays and measuring the angles with a protractor.

Incident ray

NORMAL

Reflected ray

Angle of incidence

Angle of reflection

Periscope

If you want to see over the heads of a crowd as a procession goes by you can use a periscope. A periscope is a tube with a plane mirror at either end next to a slit in the tube wall. The mirrors are set at an angle of 45 degrees to the top and bottom of the tube. When you look through the lower slit you see light that has entered the upper slit.

Kaleidoscope

A kaleidoscope is a tube with three mirrors inside it set at an angle of 60 degrees to each other. Small pieces of coloured plastic are placed between them and five images of the pieces appear in the mirrors to make an attractive pattern. This is viewed from the other end of the tube. Kaleidoscopes are used as toys today but in the past they were sometimes used by designers.

The rays of light are reflected by both mirrors in a periscope and give you a clear view which is not reversed.

mirrors

The coloured objects and five reflections make up this pattern.

Angles of incidence and reflection

An investigation was made by shining a beam of light at different angles onto a flat mirror. The data is incomplete. Predict the values of the missing angles.

Angle of incidence	Angle of reflection
	14
25	
	35
57	
	79

CURVED MIRRORS

There are two types of curved mirrors – mirrors that curve inwards and mirrors that curve outwards. Both types have uses.

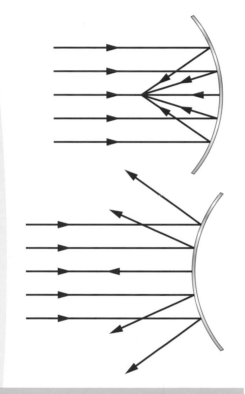

A concave mirror makes parallel rays converge.
A convex mirror makes them diverge.

Concave mirror

A concave mirror has a surface which curves inwards. When parallel rays of light strike its surface, the reflected rays come together, or converge, at a point in front of the mirror. This point is called the principal focus.

Convex mirror

A convex mirror has a surface which curves outwards. When parallel rays of light strike its surface, the reflected rays spread out, or diverge, as if they come from a point behind the mirror.

Spoon test

Hold up two metal spoons, one with the concave side towards you, and one with the convex side towards you. In the concave spoon, you will see a small upside-down image of yourself. In the convex spoon, you will see a small image of yourself which is the right way up. The sides of the spoon are like concave and convex mirrors.

Uses of concave mirrors

A concave mirror gives a magnified view of the teeth to help the dentist look for decay.

If an object is brought close to a slightly concave mirror, an image forms in the mirror which is the right way up and magnified. Concave mirrors like this are used in shaving and make-up mirrors where a magnified view of the skin is helpful. They are also used in dental mirrors to help dentists see inside your mouth more easily.

If a lamp is placed at the principal focus of some concave mirrors, the light rays from the lamp spread out and strike the mirror and their reflected rays are parallel and make a bright beam of light. Concave mirrors like this are used in torches and car headlamps.

Uses of convex mirrors

When you look in a convex mirror you can see a wide view of objects behind you. Convex mirrors are used in all kinds of motor vehicles to give the driver a wide view of traffic behind them. Convex mirrors are also used in stores in towns where they help security guards look out for people stealing goods.

The side mirrors on a car are convex and provide a wide view of traffic behind the car.

Identify the mirror

The images in four mirrors were recorded.

1 Which mirrors were concave and which were convex?
2 Which mirrors could be used as make-up mirrors?
3 Which mirrors could be used by motorists to see behind them?

Mirror	Image
A	sometimes magnified
B	wide view of image
C	sometimes upside down
D	always the right way up

THE EYE

When light rays enter the eye they are brought together to make a picture which we can see.

The parts of the eye

You can think of the eye as a bag of transparent jelly. Most of the eye wall, called the sclera, is opaque but at the front there is a transparent region. It is made up from a thin skin-like layer called the conjunctiva with a thicker layer called the cornea beneath it. Behind them is a watery material, then the coloured ring, called the iris, with the black hole, called the pupil, at its centre. Finally, behind this is the lens and the jelly which keeps the eye in shape.

Focusing light in the eye

When light rays strike the cornea they are directed to pass through the pupil. When they reach the lens their paths are turned again so that they form an image on the back wall of the eye (the retina). This changing of the path of light to make an image is called focusing. The lens becomes thick when it focuses on a close object and it becomes thin when focusing on a distant object.

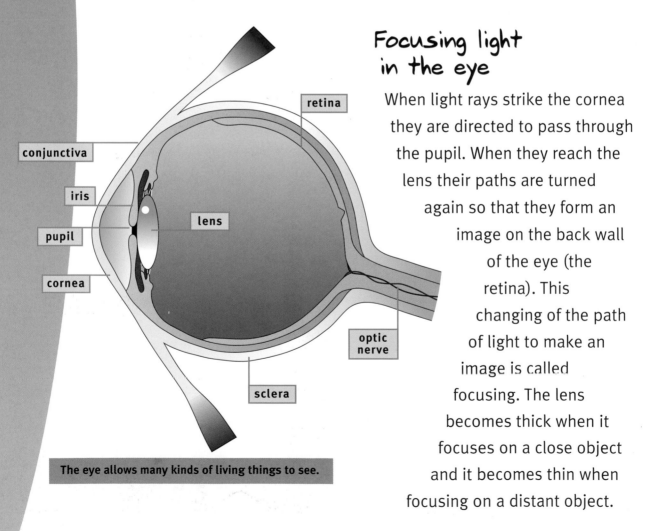

The eye allows many kinds of living things to see.

The eye and the brain

The eye is connected to the brain by the optic nerve. There are millions of endings of this nerve in the retina. When an image forms, the nerve endings send tiny electric currents along the optic nerve to the brain. Inside the brain, these tiny currents give us the sensation of seeing what the eye is looking at.

The near point

If you move this page closer to your eye, it reaches a point where the words look blurred. The nearest place to your eye where things can be seen clearly is called the near point. The near point changes as you get older.

Find your near point by seeing how close you can hold this book to your eyes and still read it.

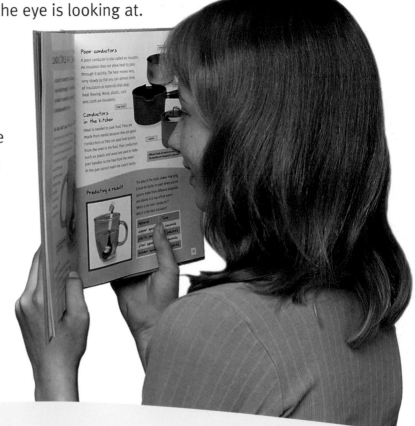

Near point and age

Here is a graph of the near points of people of different ages.

1 How does the distance of the near point change with age?
2 Use the graph to find the near point of a person who is 30.
3 Use the graph to find the age of someone whose near point is 35 cm.

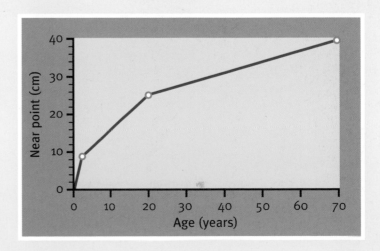

EYES AND LIGHT

Eyes are adapted to dealing with different amounts of light.

Light and sight

Our eyes allow us to see if a certain amount of light enters them. If too little light enters them, everything is dark and we cannot see. If too much light enters them, we are dazzled and again we cannot see.

The iris and pupil

The amount of light entering the eye is controlled by the iris. It is made from two sets of muscles. One set, called radial muscles, are arranged like spokes in a bicycle wheel. The other set, called the circular muscles, are arranged in circles, one inside the other. The muscles pull to make changes. When one set pulls they contract, or get shorter, and the other set relaxes and become longer. When the radial muscles pull, they make the pupil wider and more light enters the eye. When the circular muscles pull, they make the pupil smaller and less light enters the eye.

From light to dark

When you move from a light place to a dark place the radial muscles pull and make the pupil larger. More light can enter your eye and form an image on the retina.

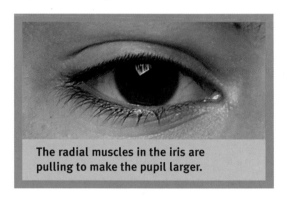

The radial muscles in the iris are pulling to make the pupil larger.

From dark to light

When you move from a dark place to a light place the circular muscles pull and make the pupil smaller. Less light enters your eye to form an image on the retina.

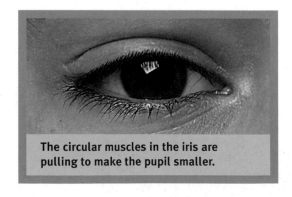

The circular muscles in the iris are pulling to make the pupil smaller.

Nocturnal animals

Animals that are active at night are called nocturnal animals. Many have large eyes with very wide pupils so as much light as possible can enter them. During the day the pupils almost close so just a little light can enter.

At night the pupils of this bush baby open wide to let it see in the dark.

Pupils and light intensity

A person moves through four places but some of the data about light intensity and pupil change has not been recorded. Fill in the gaps.

	Light intensity	Pupil change
Sunny park	increase	
Dark cinema		increase
Bright cafe	increase	
Street at night		increase

COLOUR

The light from the Sun and most electric lamps is called white light. It is made up from seven different colours of light. The way these colours are absorbed and reflected let us see the world in colour.

Forming a spectrum

When a beam of white light is shone into the side of a prism at a certain angle, coloured beams of light come out the other side. They can make a series of coloured bands called a spectrum on a screen. This spreading out of coloured light is called dispersion.

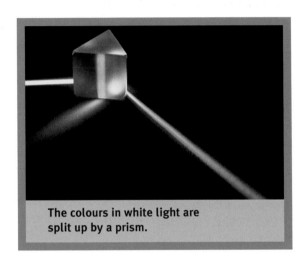

The colours in white light are split up by a prism.

The rainbow

You can see a rainbow when sunlight shines from behind you into a rain cloud. The cloud is made of millions of water droplets. When the white light enters them it is dispersed and the colours are reflected. All the reflected coloured light makes the rainbow.

The water droplets in the cloud disperse the seven colours in sunlight to make a rainbow.

Colours in objects

When white light strikes an object, the colours in the light can be reflected or absorbed. If all the colours are reflected, we see the object as white. If all the colours are absorbed, we see the object as black due to an absence of light. Coloured objects absorb some colours and reflect others. For example, a red object reflects red but absorbs all the other colours.

Coloured filters

A coloured filter is a transparent material with a substance in it which absorbs most colours and only allows one colour to pass through. For example, a red filter contains a material which absorbs all the colours in white light except red and so lets red light pass through it.

We see the colours of everything on the stage by the light reflected from the stage lights.

Sky colours and scattering

The air contains huge amounts of dust. When white light from the Sun passes through it, some of the blue light is scattered by the dust and this makes the sky blue. Clouds are made of water droplets. When white light enters a cloud the droplets scatter it in all directions. This makes the clouds appear white.

Coloured filters

The seven colours in white light are red, orange, yellow, green, blue, indigo and violet.

1 What colours are absorbed by an object we see as red?

2 What colour is reflected by an object we see as green?

3 What colours cannot pass through a blue filter?

4 If light shines though a red filter, and then a green one, why does no light pass through the second filter?

CAN YOU REMEMBER THE ESSENTIALS?

Here are the essential science facts about light and seeing. They are set out in the order you can read about them in the book. Spend a couple of minutes learning each set of facts. If you can learn them all, you will know all the essentials about the science of light and seeing.

Sources of light (pages 6—7)

Objects which give out light are called light sources or luminous objects.
The Sun and stars are luminous objects.
Burning objects are luminous.
Electric lamps and TV and computer screens are luminous objects.
Objects which do not give out light are non-luminous objects.

Shadows (pages 10—11)

A shadow forms when light is stopped by an opaque object.
A shadow is dark because light is absent.
Light cannot bend round objects.
The length of the shadow depends on the height of the light source shining on the object.

When light travels (pages 8—9)

Light travels in straight lines.
A pinhole camera can be used to make a picture of a luminous object.
Light travels at 300,000 metres per second.

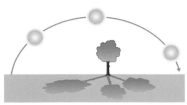

Shadows and time (pages 12—13)

Shadows cast by objects in sunlight can be used to tell the time.
The movement of the Sun in the sky is really due to the way the Earth turns round.
Shadows can be used to show directions.
The sundial and Sun bar are two devices used to tell the time by using shadows.

Materials and light (pages 14–15)

Opaque materials do not let light pass through them.
Transparent materials let light pass through them so that objects can be clearly seen on the other side.
Translucent materials let some light pass through them but objects on the other side cannot be clearly seen.

The eye (Pages 22–23)

Light passes into the transparent front of the eye.
Light rays are focused by the lens.
An image of the view is made on the retina inside the eye.
The optic nerve sends information about the image to the brain.
The brain gives us the sensation of seeing.

Reflecting light (pages 16–17)

A beam of light is made up from many thin parallel light rays.
Rough surfaces give diffuse reflections where no images can be seen.
Smooth, flat surfaces give specular reflections in which images can be seen.
In a mirror image, left and right are reversed.

Eyes and light (pages 24–25)

The eye can control how much light enters it.
Light enters the inside of the eye through the pupil.
The size of the pupil is controlled by the muscles in the iris.
The pupil is large in dim light and small in bright light.
Nocturnal animals have large eyes.

Flat mirrors (pages 18–19)

Flat mirrors are also called plane mirrors.
In flat mirrors, the angle of incidence is the same as the angle of reflection.
A periscope has two plane mirrors and can be used to see over the top of a crowd.
A kaleidoscope has three plane mirrors and can be used to make attractive patterns.

Colour (pages 26–27)

A prism can split up white light into light of seven colours.
Water droplets in clouds can split up sunlight to make a rainbow.
Objects absorb some colours and reflect others.
The colour of an object is the colour it reflects.
A filter absorbs all colours of light except one and allows that colour to pass through it.

Curved mirrors (pages 20–21)

A concave mirror has a surface that curves inwards.
A convex mirror has a surface that curves outwards.
A concave mirror gives an upside-down image but, close up, it can make a magnified image, which is the right way up.
A convex mirror gives a wide view, the right way up.

GLOSSARY

Angle of incidence The angle measured from the normal to the path of a ray of light striking a surface.

Angle of reflection The angle measured from the normal to the path of a ray of light that is reflected from a surface.

Astronomer A person who studies objects in space such as stars, planets and moons.

Auditorium The part of a theatre or cinema in which the audience sits.

Axis A line running through the centre of the Earth from the North to the South Pole.

Bush baby A small nocturnal animal found in Africa. They have large round eyes and big ears.

Concave A surface which curves inwards.

Convex A surface which curves outwards.

Conductor A material which allows electricity to pass easily through it.

Cornea The transparent front part of the eye.

Diffuse reflections These occur when the rays of reflected light spread out in all directions.

Energy Something which allows an object or a living thing to take part in an activity.

Hemisphere Either the northern or southern half of the Earth.

Incident ray The light ray that strikes a surface.

Lens A transparent object with curved surfaces which changes the path of light as it passes through it.

Light meter An electrical device with a light sensor and a scale for measuring the amount of light in a place.

Light year The distance travelled by a ray of light in a year. A light year is almost 9.5 million million kilometres.

Normal (the) A line that is at right angles to a surface where light rays are being reflected.

Opaque object An object through which light rays cannot pass.

Oxygen A gas in the air which does not have any colour or smell.

Parallel lines Lines which are side by side and have the same distance between them all along their length.

Prism A solid object with two triangular sides separated by three rectangular sides.

Reflected ray The light ray which leaves a surface after an incident ray has struck it.

Resistance A property of a conductor to slow down the flow of electricity through it.

Retina The light-sensitive surface at the back of the eye.

Specular reflections These occur when rays of reflected light travel in parallel lines.

Translucent material A material which scatters light in all directions as it passes through it.

Transparent material A material which allows light to pass straight though it.

ANSWERS

Sources of light (pages 6—7)

1 Mirphak, Hamal, Mebsuta, Sheliak, Mira.
2 Mira.

When light travels (pages 8—9)

1 The year sixteen years ago.
2 The year 1,800 years from now.
3 268 light years.

Shadows (pages 10—11)

1 (a) 10 cm, (b) 7 cm.
2 30 cm.
3 Longer.

Shadows and time (pages 12—13)

1

East	50	West
South east	40	North west
South	25	North
South west	40	North east
West	50	East

2 The Northern Hemisphere.

Materials and light (pages 14—15)

1 B.
2 A.
3 C
4 C.

Reflecting light (pages 16—17)

Surface	Reflection (yes/no)
This book cover	yes
This page	no
Polished metal	yes
Wool pullover	no

Flat mirrors (pages 18—19)

Angle of incidence	Angle or reflection
14	14
25	25
35	35
57	57
79	79

Curved mirrors (pages 20—21)

1 Concave A, C; Convex B, D
2 A, C.
3 B, D.

The eye (Pages 22—23)

1 It increases with age.
2 28 cm.
3 60.

The eyes and light (pages 24—25)

	Light intensity	Pupil change
A	Increase	Decrease
B	Decrease	Increase
C	Increase	Decrease
D	Decrease	Increase

Colour (pages 26—27)

1 Orange, yellow, green, blue, indigo and violet.
2 Green.
3 Red, orange, yellow, green, indigo and violet.
4 Only red light passes through the red filter and it cannot get through the green filter.

INDEX